R Is for Reparations
Young Activists Speaking Their Truth

Global Afrikan Congress – Nova Scotia Chapter
with the Book-in-a-Day Children

Edited by C. Denise Gillard

Roseway Publishing
Halifax & Winnipeg

In February 2018, 30 children aged 7 to 12 from the Municipality of Halifax, Nova Scotia, came together and wrote this book in one day. That's right! A Book-in-a-Day! How did they do it? They divided into groups and boarded the imaginary Reparations Freedom Train. All Aboard! Grown-up "conductors" took them from station to station. At each stop, there was a stationmaster artist to help them express social justice thoughts, feelings and movements. These artists helped them discover their views on the topic of reparations. This alphabet book is made of their art and words. We hope that when you read this book, you will join them on the journey towards reparations too.

For the Atlantic Slave Trade, Slavery, and Colonialism
And the lasting legacy of discrimination, poverty, and anti-Black racism—
Every European and Western nation must admit and apologize
For this crime against humanity and our foreparents' cries.
We must be paid for the work we have done.
We will not stop until payment for damages is won.
We claim our right to the interest earned—
On the people and the riches that were stolen and spurned.
Our rightful inheritance to wholeness, health, and joy.
A positive outlook for every Black girl and every Black boy.
Reparations for Afrikan people is what we want today.
We, the children, are leading the way!

All Aboard! It's time to hop on the Reparations Freedom Train.
You don't need money.
You don't need luggage.
All you need is the courage to speak your truth and make your demands for social justice.
All you need is the alphabet to find your words.
R is for *Re-pa-ra-tions*! Reparations is what we want and we want it now.

Get ready! The train is pulling out of the station. Get ready. Get set. Let's Go!
— Denise Gillard, editor

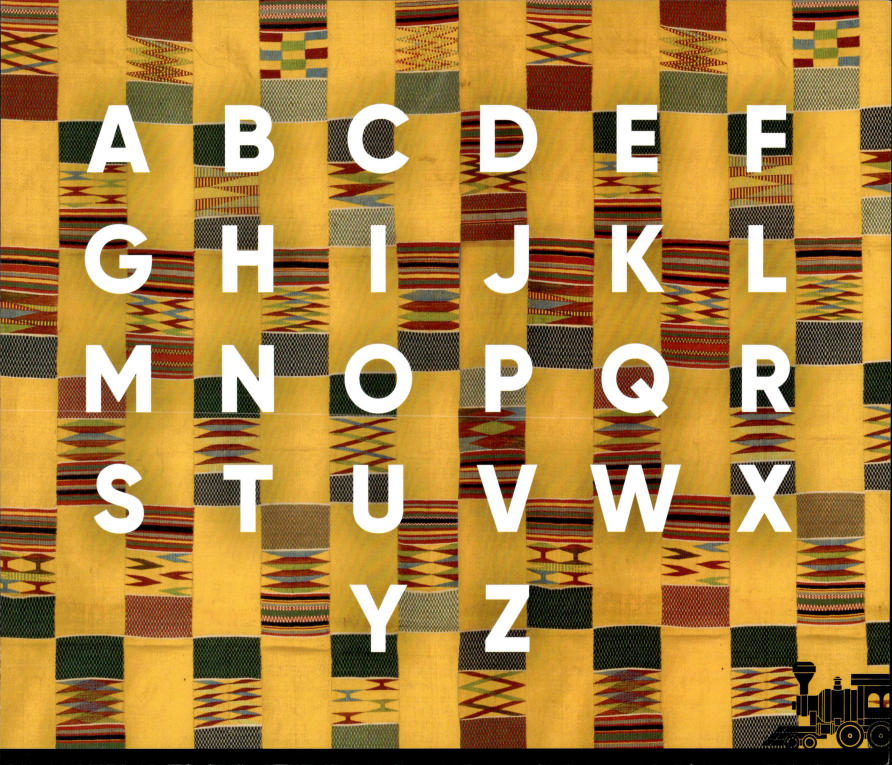

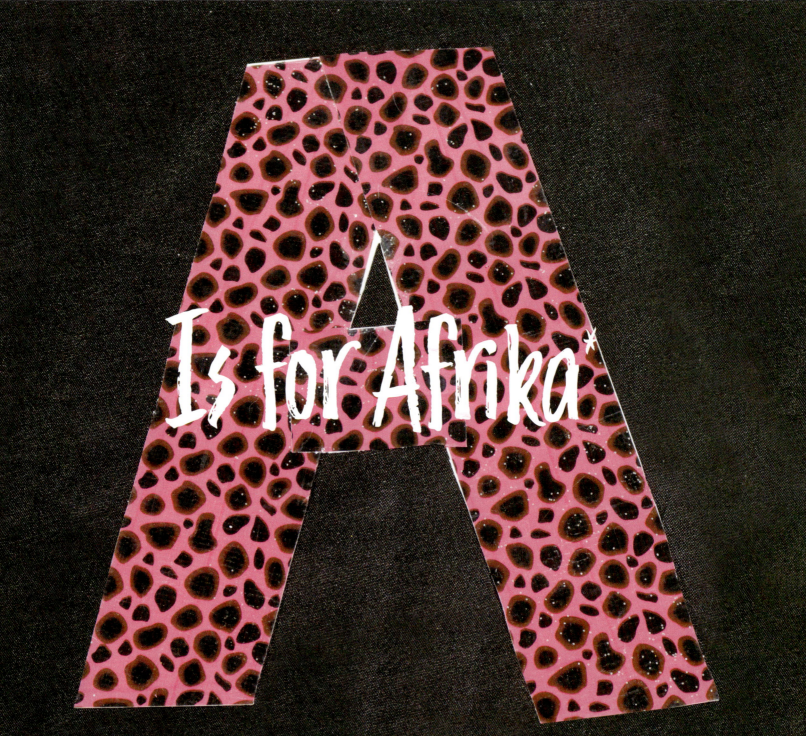

Afrika is where Black people are from. **Afrika** is where all people come from. I am demanding something so I spell **Afrika** the way my people did. **Afrika** is my home.

When I say **Afrika**, I think of **Africville**. When I think of **Africville***, I think of what was taken. We were robbed.

They took our lives, our food, our money, our uncles.

A Is for Activism

I **am active** for **Afrika**!

I **am active** for Reparations!

Ashay!*

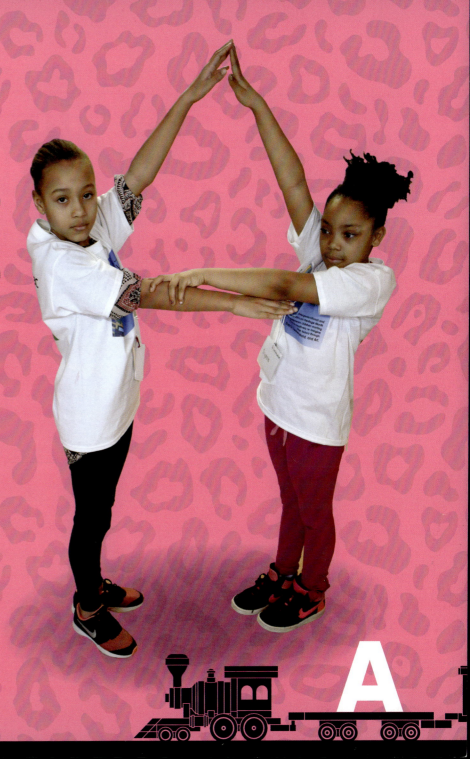

Is for Black People

Strong, **beautiful Black** people with **beautiful** hair.

We want to **Be**.

We want to **be** treated as humans!
Being human means not **being** treated like animals.

Being together, **being** safe, **being** happy.
Not **being** afraid of anything.

We want to **be** free!

Not **being** judged by the colour of our skin.

No **barriers**, no **bad** words, and no **banning** immigrants!

No more **building** walls **between** people! No **bullying**!

Everyone **belongs**!

I **belong** and I want my things **back**!

Ashay!

C Is for Cause

I have a **cause**!

Countless children who look like me are **crying**.

That's a **crime**! We demand money, food, home, and family.

Criminals stole our families and our languages.

They **came** with dogs, and we got robbed and **cheated**. We had to work without pay in the sun.

We are **children** of God. **Children** of the sea and **children** of the earth.

We are a **community** that will **continue**.

We will **cause** you to **care**!

Ashay!

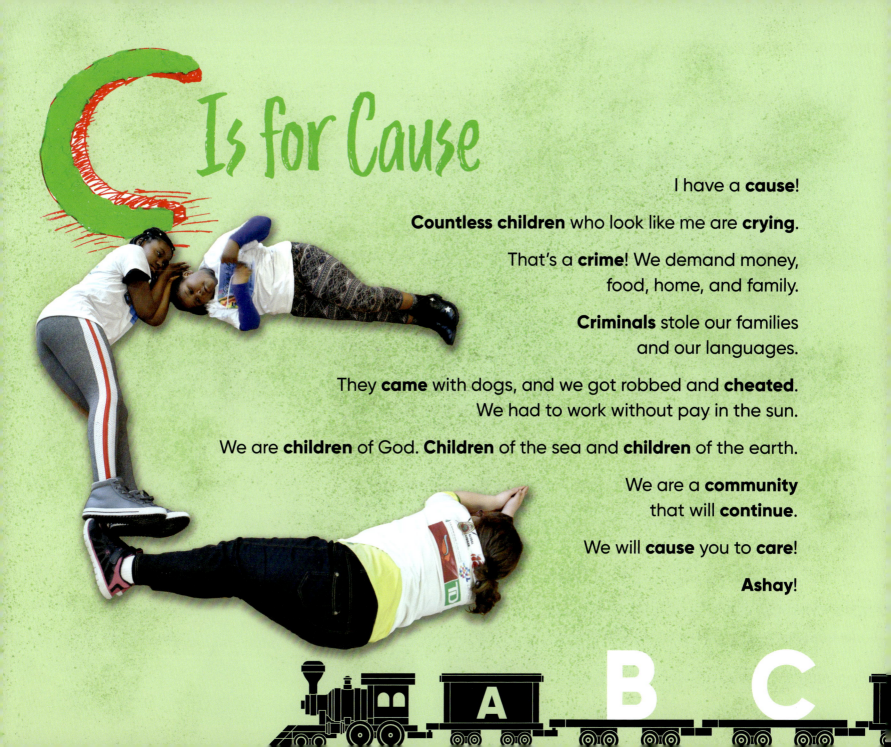

Is for Demand

As an activist, I am **determined** to **demand** reparations for **damage done** to my people.

You must **do** something when someone makes you **do** something without a return.

When someone treats you like **dirt** or puts you in **danger**, then you **discover** what you are made of.

Do we want to give up?

Sometimes, maybe, but we have the **determination** to **do** the right thing.

If we work together, we will get the work **done** quicker.

Ashay!

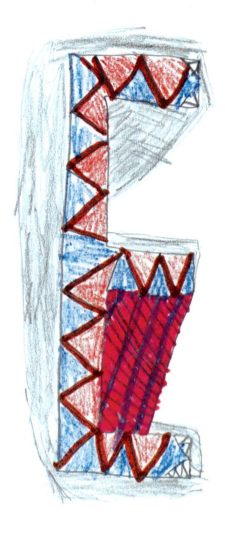

Is for Expectation

Each and **every** day we need to **examine** our hearts and **educate** our minds.

We must **eliminate** the lies told on us.

We are an **effective** people.

We are **excellent**. We bring **excitement**. We have **endurance**.

The **economy** of **European** society was built on our **energy**.

We are full of **expectation**! We **expect** the bill to be paid.

Enough is **enough**!

Ashay!

F Is for Fearless

I will not **fear**! I will speak up and that's a **fact**!

F Is for Family, Friends, and Faith

I love my **family** and **friends**. My **family** believes in me.

F Is for Freedom

You are not **free** if someone takes you and **forces** you to do things for them.

I am **free**, not enslaved.

F is for the **forgiveness** needed to stop killing and end wars. We **forgive** wrongdoers who give back the things they took.

I am not asking for a **favour**. Do you **feel** me?

Ashay!

G Is for Good and Global and Governments

The people in charge all over the world should be **good** to all people.

There is a **global** need for **governments** to **get** things right! They need to be **grateful** that they **get** to lead.

Everybody needs the chance to **grow**. Everybody deserves a **good** life on this earth. **Globalization** of the **good**!

No **gun** shots where we live.

Life is not a **game**!

Ashay!

H Is for Human

Human beings are not animals.
We were not created for whipping.

I am a **human** being. I am smart.
I am talented. I am me.

I can **help**. I can **help** the environment.

I can **help** someone be **happy**.

I am **honourable**. My **history** is **honourable**.

I will not **hesitate** to talk about what I need to be **happy**.

I **hope** you **hear** me. You must **hear** me!

Ashay!

Is for Important

I am **important**! Me, myself, and **I**.

I want to get our languages back.
I want money and a new home.

I demand my **inheritance**. **I** want peace.

I could travel or buy a car or a truck to do something **important**.

I am **impactful**—full of **impact** and very **intelligent**. Actually, **I'm irresistible**!

I would fix things by signing an **international** peace treaty.

I would protect the **innocent**.

I need you and you need me.

Ashay!

J Is for Justice

Martin Luther King, **Jr**. and Viola Desmond brought **justice** to people who were not treated fairly.

Justice means doing the right things even when others are **just** doing the wrong things.

Just because you are a little girl or a boy doesn't mean you can't tell people to stop hating and killing.

Justice is supposed to be for everyone.

It's a **journey**.

Join us!

Ashay!

K Is for Knowledge

Knowledge is the **key** to freedom.

We need to **know** the **key** to breathing and being healthy. We need to **know** how to survive. We need to **know** how to build stuff and pay our bills.

Knowledge builds wealth.

K Is for Kujichagulia*

Kujichagulia lets me **know** that I can define and name myself. **Kujichagulia** lets the world **know** that I will create stuff and speak for myself.

I **know** my rights!

Do you want to **know** me?

Ashay!

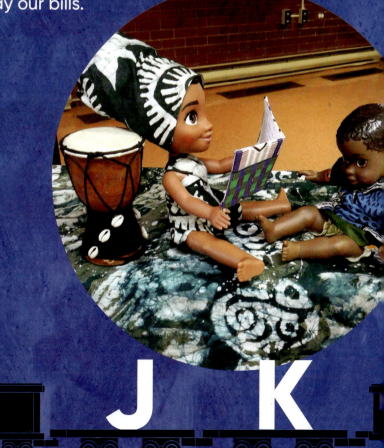

Is for Love

We must **love** one and **love** all.

Love means taking action to make things right for everyone in the **land** of Canada and all over the world.

You must open your eyes to see what people **lost**.

I think the **law** should make people accept responsibility for the **lasting legacy** of the bad things.

Reparations are my **legal** right.

Ashay!

M Is for Money

Money does not grow on trees — you have to earn it.

When I earn **money**, I will use it to help the poor, give **money** to organizations, and donate to important **matters**.

You can do a lot with twenty dollars. You can do **more** with a **million**.

My **mind** is **made** up to help the homeless before I shop.

We want to know where the **money** is for all the work our ancestors did. We demand payment.

M Is for Mother

My mother is **marvellous**. She gave birth to **me** and gives **me** food.

Afrika is **my Motherland**.

Ashay!

Is for No!

I say **No**! **No** bad things!

No arguing! **No** racism! **No** drugs!

No stealing, **no** head-lice, **no** ticks!

No to lying. **Never** lie.

No telling people they are ugly.

Negative words put people down. **Now** is the time to change.

We **need** change.

Sometimes you just **need** to say **No**!

Ashay!

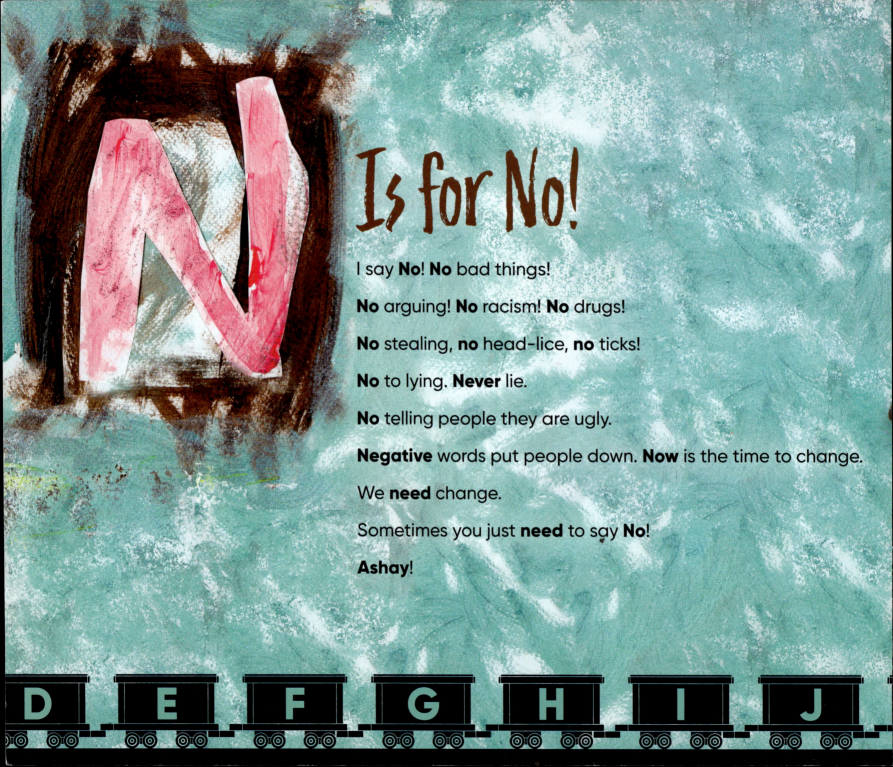

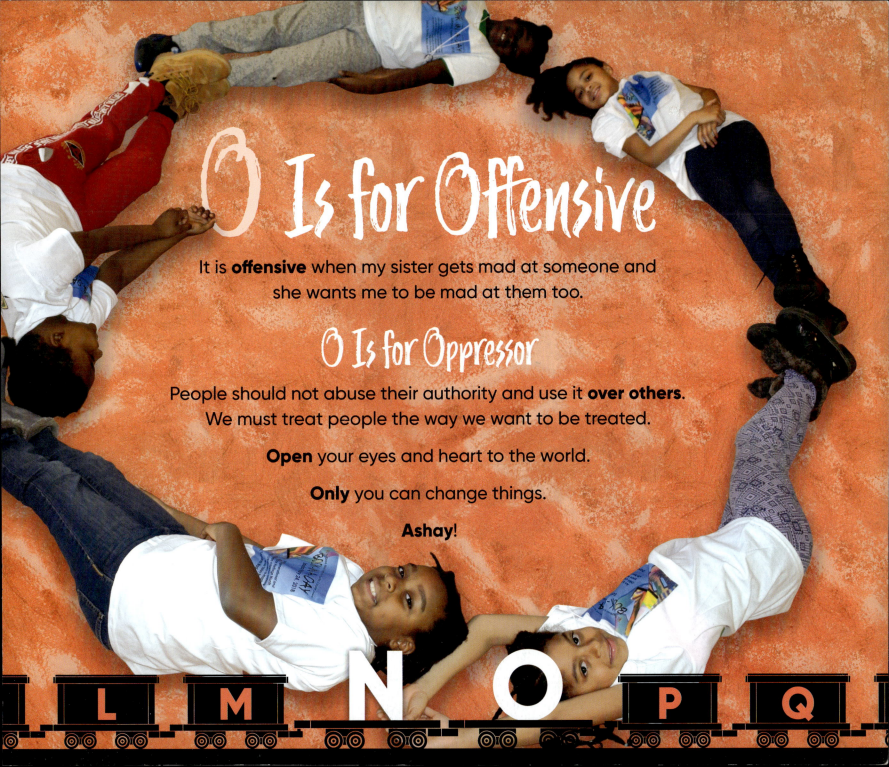

O Is for Offensive

It is **offensive** when my sister gets mad at someone and she wants me to be mad at them too.

O Is for Oppressor

People should not abuse their authority and use it **over others**. We must treat people the way we want to be treated.

Open your eyes and heart to the world.

Only you can change things.

Ashay!

L M N O P Q

P Is for People

"**People** get ready, there's a train a comin'."

Pack your baggage up. **Please** don't carry your hurts around.

You are **powerful** enough to let go of the things that weigh you down.

Your hands are **powerful**.
Your words are **powerful**.

Be **positive**.

You just need to be **persistent**, **prayerful**, and **purposeful**.

You have **possibilities**!

Ashay!

H I J K L M N

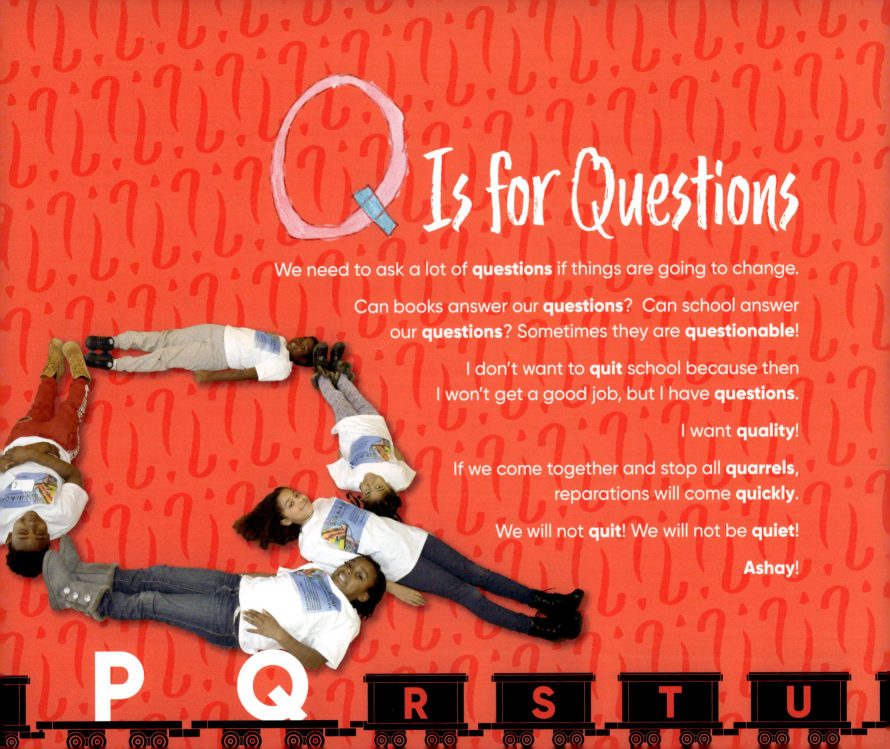

Q Is for Questions

We need to ask a lot of **questions** if things are going to change.

Can books answer our **questions**? Can school answer our **questions**? Sometimes they are **questionable**!

I don't want to **quit** school because then I won't get a good job, but I have **questions**.

I want **quality**!

If we come together and stop all **quarrels**, reparations will come **quickly**.

We will not **quit**! We will not be **quiet**!

Ashay!

R Is for Reparations

K L M N O P Q

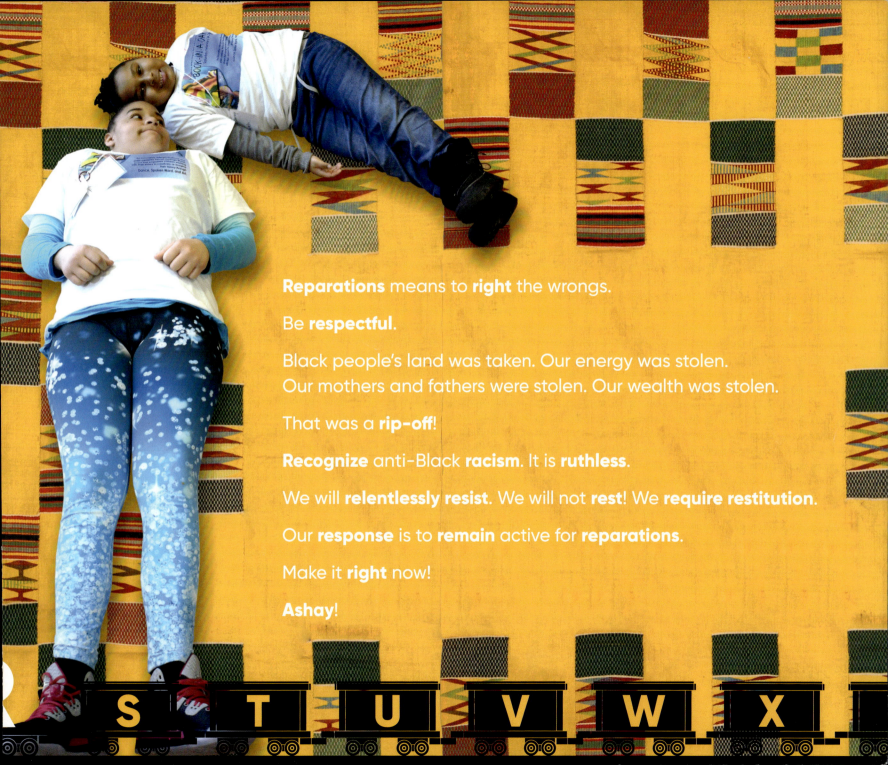

Reparations means to **right** the wrongs.

Be **respectful**.

Black people's land was taken. Our energy was stolen.
Our mothers and fathers were stolen. Our wealth was stolen.

That was a **rip-off**!

Recognize anti-Black **racism**. It is **ruthless**.

We will **relentlessly resist**. We will not **rest**! We **require restitution**.

Our **response** is to **remain** active for **reparations**.

Make it **right** now!

Ashay!

S Is for Stop

Stop is a **strong** word.

Stop taking advantage.

Stop killing.

Somebody made a **sacrifice** for you.

It's really **simple**.

You are **somebody**, and a better world **starts** with you.

This is **straight** talk!

Ashay!

T Is for Taking the Time

Take the time to treat people nicely.

Stay out of **trouble**.

It is **tremendous** to accomplish something **through the truth**.

You could be famous—a designer or actor and be **trusted to** do great **things**.

Show **thankfulness**.

Teach somebody what it **takes to** succeed.

Pass **the test**.

You need to have a **testimony**.

It **takes teamwork**.

So, **take** back your power.

Ashay!

U Is for Unity

We are a **united** people.

We are **unselfish** and **uncompromising**.

Does that make you **uncomfortable**?

Don't **underestimate** us.

Don't be **unjust**.

Undo the bad.

We are telling the world about our **urgent** needs.

Urgency happens when you're late for something. That is **unacceptable**.

We must be **understood**!

Ashay!

V Is for Valuable

It is **very** important that I **value** myself.

V Is for Vision

Be a **victor**, not a **victim**! **Victory** is mine!

V Is for Vocalize

I am a **voice** for the **voiceless**.
I will not **vanish**!

Ashay!

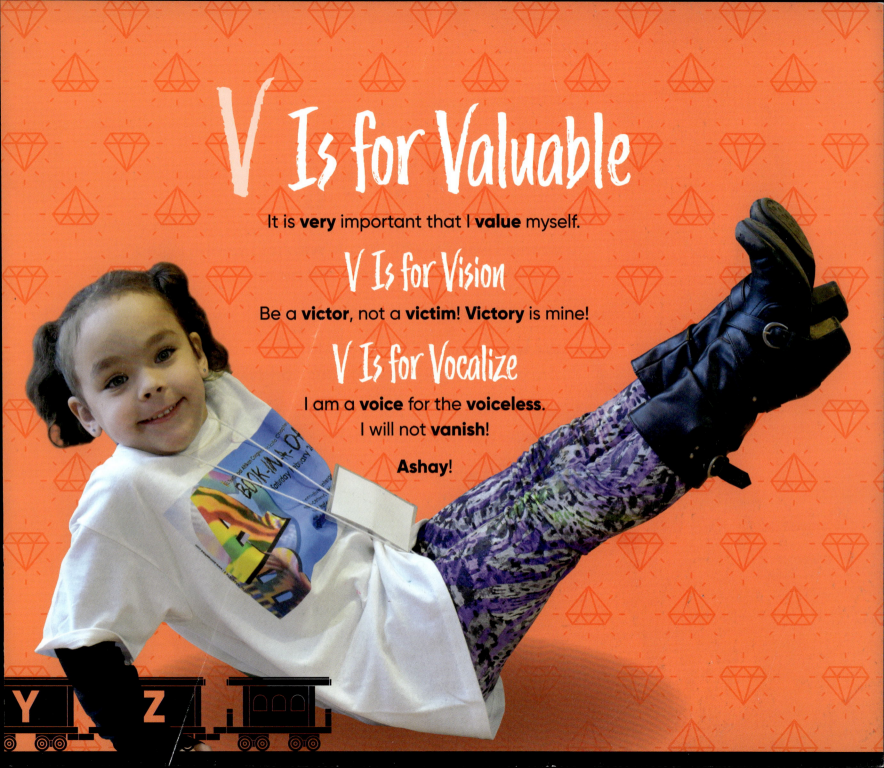

Is for Wrong

White privilege is **wrong**! **White** supremacy and **world** domination are **wrong**! I **wonder why** people **withhold wealth** instead of using **wisdom** to make the **world** better.

God is **watching** us and **waiting** to see if **we will work** together.

We want the best for the **world**.
Are you **willing** to change your **worldview**?

We call on all levels of government from all over the **world** to **wake** up.

We won't whisper! Our power is **within**.

We will win!

Ashay!

X Is for Malcolm X

They stole his name
so he made his own.

Don't even try to **X** me out.

I won't allow my ideas to be **exploited**.

I will not let my dreams be **extinguished**.

Each one of us needs to **examine** ourselves before we **exit** this world.

Ashay!

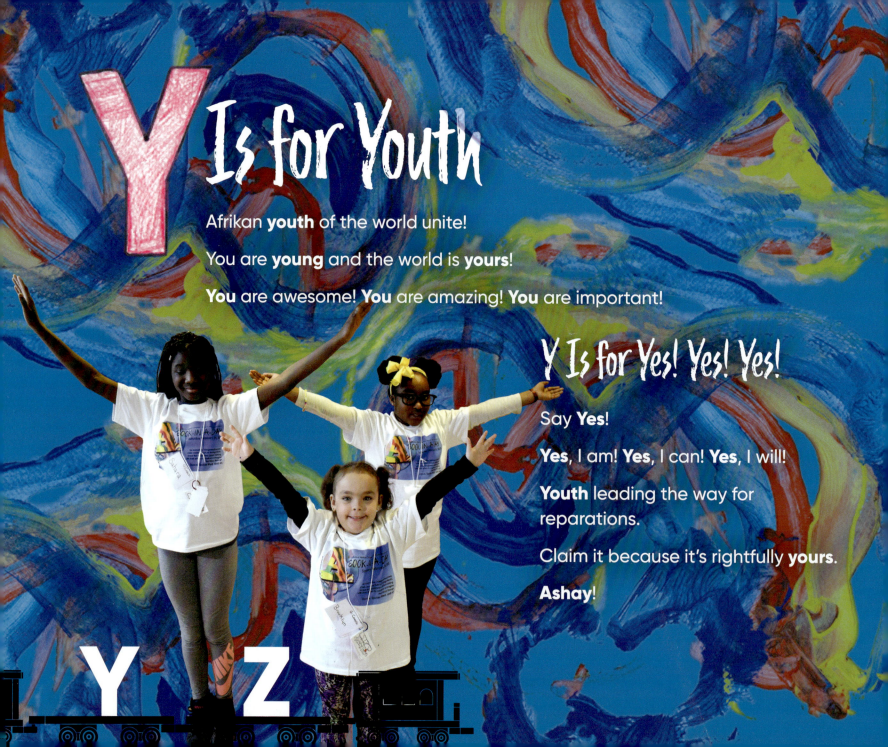

Y Is for Youth

Afrikan **youth** of the world unite!

You are **young** and the world is **yours**!

You are awesome! **You** are amazing! **You** are important!

Y Is for Yes! Yes! Yes!

Say **Yes**!

Yes, I am! **Yes**, I can! **Yes**, I will!

Youth leading the way for reparations.

Claim it because it's rightfully **yours**.

Ashay!

Y   Z

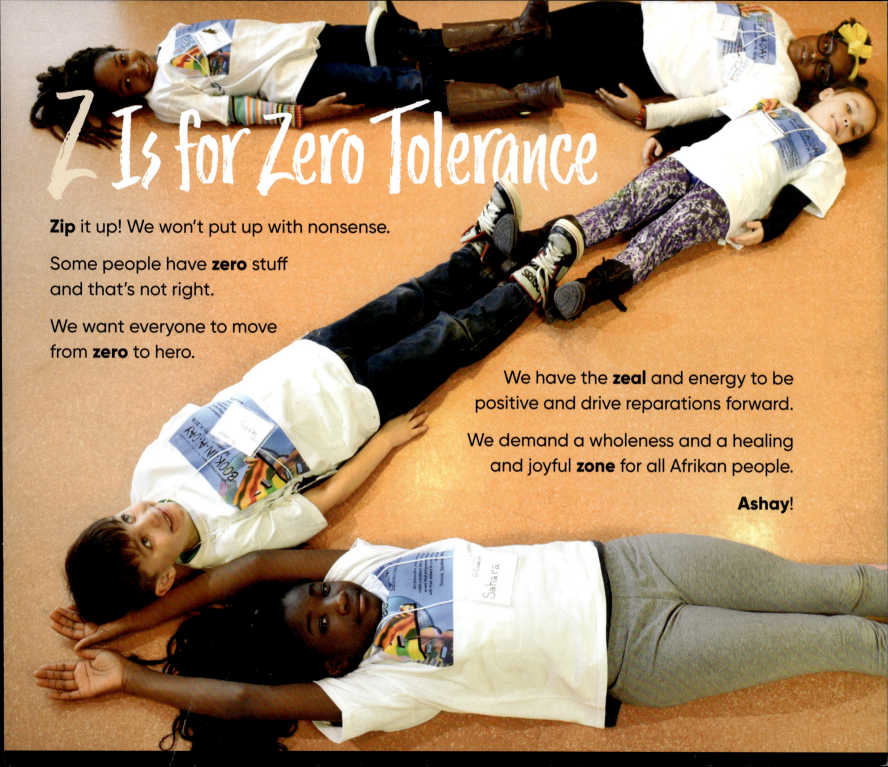

Z Is for Zero Tolerance

Zip it up! We won't put up with nonsense.

Some people have **zero** stuff and that's not right.

We want everyone to move from **zero** to hero.

We have the **zeal** and energy to be positive and drive reparations forward.

We demand a wholeness and a healing and joyful **zone** for all Afrikan people.

Ashay!

Glossary

Afrika

We spell the name "Afrika" with "k" as oppsed to "c" because:

- it is a Pan-Afrikan spelling which relates both to the Afrikan continent and the Diaspora
- it reflects the spelling of "Afrika" in all Afrikan languages
- it includes the concept of "ka," the vital energy which both sustains and creates life, as expressed in ancient Kemetic (Egyptian) teachings.

The terms "Afrikan" and "Black" in this book, refer to the indigenous people of Afrika and their descendants throughout the Diaspora, in all corners of the world.

Africville

A community on the southern shore of the Bedford Basin, in Halifax, Nova Scotia, which was founded largely by formerly enslaved people from the United States who were freed following the American Revolution and the War of 1812. During the 20th century, the city of Halifax introduced a variety of undesired and unhealthy industrial services to the community, but did not provide the services enjoyed by all other tax payers such as fire services, sanitation, and clean water. In the 1960s, under the heading of "urban renewal," the city relocated the whole of Africville against the residents' wishes. In 2010, the city of Halifax issued a formal apology to the former residents and descendants of Africville. Many residents are still seeking justice for the wrongs up to present day. (Courtesy of *Juanita Peters, General Manager at Africville Museum*)

Ashay

The word Ase, Ashe or Ashay is from the Yoruba (Nigerian) àṣẹ or axé. This is the West Afrikan belief that tells Afrikan people that we have the power to bring change and make things happen. Dr. Guracha Clem Marshall—author of *Talking Cheddo: Liberating PanAfrikanism*—describes it as "calling on the Ancestors to come to our aid, give us the energy to fix whatever had gone wrong and put our world back in balance" and explains that although the spelling can change among Black populations it always sounds the same. It is a "precious, powerful word that our Ancestors passed down to us."

Kujichagulia

Say it like this: *koo-jee-cha-goo-LEE-ah*. It is the Afrikan Swahili word for self-determination.

Note to Educators, Community Leaders, Parents & Guardians

"It's time for a centuries-overdue discussion about Canada's legacy of slavery, its lasting harms on Black Canadians and potential forms of reparation."
—Global Afrikan Congress – Nova Scotia Chapter

The Global Afrikan Congress (GAC) is an international organization that was established by, for, and on behalf of Afrikans on the continent and in the Diaspora. The organization offers an opportunity for solidarity, cooperation, and empowerment and a viable means for Afrikan people throughout the world to work towards common objectives and to foster value in and respect for the diversity of the Afrikan family.

The Global Afrikan Congress – Nova Scotia Chapter (GAC-NS) was established in 2010 and throughout its history has provided a strong and forceful voice for Afrikan people advocating for justice in the form of reparations for victims of the Atlantic Slave Trade and colonization and the crime against humanity.

The uniqueness of the geographical area and its distinct people (Nova Scotia being the birthplace of the indigenous Afrikan people of Canada, who arrived in the early 1600s) has prompted the GAC-NS to ensure the history of the area and all of its people are included in any discourse on reparations on the Canadian and global stage.

In February 2018, the GAC-NS facilitated an innovative Book-in-a-Day event, which combined instruction, facilitation, and creative/artistic components to support children from the Halifax area in contributing materials for an alphabet book centred on the topic of reparations. The premise behind this endeavour was that an alphabet book-in-a-day would satisfy the children's need to tell their own story of reparations and have a visible end product since their book would be easily understood and produced in a timely manner by and for them. This endeavour along with the GAC's goal of engaging everyone in the call for "reparations now" proved itself a good match to advance the reparations agenda.

Reparations is the global demand for redress, compensation, and restitution that addresses the tragedy and resulting political, social, and economic damage caused to Afrikan People by the Atlantic Slave Trade, slavery, and colonialism, including its lasting legacy of poverty, discrimination, and anti-Black racism. European and Western nations must acknowledge and apologize for this crime against humanity inflicted upon Afrikan people and engage in a process to provide the necessary reparations (GAC definition).

Most of the children who participated in Book-in-a-Day had never heard the word **reparations** before but once engaged through an imaginary Reparations Freedom Train equipped with elders who served as "conductors" and "station" stops which used various art forms to facilitate learning and sharing, the children led the discussion and created the materials for this one-of-a-kind book. When you read this book, you join them on a reparations freedom train journey which is in alignment with the Twelve Fundamental Principles articulated in *The Reparations Manifesto*:

1. Validation of our humanity
2. Knowledge of our history
3. Completion of the emancipation process
4. Compensation must be proportionate to the crime
5. Reparations must produce the just society
6. No one must be left behind
7. Africans must exercise autonomy throughout the process
8. We must repair ourselves
9. Self-repair will generate mass support for reparations
10. Reparations must be a broad movement
11. The mass of our people must be intimately involved
12. Network and establish a new international legal structure

In the words of David Comissiong, Chairman Caribbean Pan-African Network (CPAN):

The time has come for the African and African descendant people of the world and their governments to finally present their Reparations Bill to the current day successor governments of those national governments of Europe and North America that organized, facilitated, legitimized, financed, and benefited from the trans-Atlantic Slave Trade and the associated system of racialized Chattel Slavery—the governments of Britain, Spain, France, Portugal, Holland, Belgium, Denmark, Germany, Canada, Sweden, Norway, and the United States of America (a former colony that perpetuated the enslavement of African people for nearly one hundred years after attaining its independence). Let us mobilize ourselves and march onwards like a mighty Army to the achievement of Reparations in this United Nations International Decade for People of African Descent!

Ashay!

Authors

Children *(we apologize for any errors or omissions)*
Neime Ada; Jaya Anderson; Onafalujo Atinuke; Abena Atwell-Rodney; Jorga-Rain Cain; Yolanden Cain; Brooklyn Clarke; Amaris Colley; Keenan Colley; Trayah Cyr; Cortel Downey; Cindy Fahey; Derwin Jackson; Dwayne Jackson; Dwight Jackson; Jayla Johnston-Curran; Jordyn Johnston-Curran; Niala Jones; Leo Klassen; Zya Langdon; Theodore Le Page; Temitope Olatunji; Joliyah Regan; Cairo Simmons-Benard; Sahora Simmons-Benard; Amaris Symonds; Amara Tie; Chika Tie; DeCosta Thomas; Ja'Quel Upshaw; Siyasia Upshaw-Allison; Tia Upshaw-Paris; Lenai White

GAC Committee Members
Lynn Jones; Wendy Shea; Wanda Thomas; Norma Williams

Project Director and Editor
Rev Denise Gillard, My Divine Appointment

Facilitators
Reader's Theatre Storyteller: Gail Teixeira
Arts and Crafts Facilitators: Mary Lekea-Ogaa & Kim Cain
Dance Facilitator: Kyla Simmons
Photographers: Wanda Taylor & Sarah Taylor
Storyteller Facilitator: Nathan Simmons
Spoken Word Facilitator: El Jones

Recorders
Recorder Artist: Othell Downey
Lead Recording Coordinator and Social Media Recorder: Tiffany Gorden
Recording Team: Nenyo Kwasitou & Rita Ugbebor

Valuable Volunteers
Mary Byard; Kenneth Cassidy; Cynamon Downey; Nicole Fountain; Evetta Thomas

Caterer
Charlotte's Sensational Taste Catering

Reparations Freedom Train Art
Denise Gillard

Special Acknowledgements
A heartfelt thanks to Amos Kennedy, Master Printer who travelled from Detroit, Michigan, to support the children in designing their own personalized event posters for the book launch, and Samantha Walkes, Black and beautiful star of the Neptune Theatre's production of *Cinderella* who graced the children with her joyful presence encouraging them to be their very best.

Sponsors
TD Bank Group
African Nova Scotian Affairs
Communities, Culture and
    Heritage, Nova Scotia
CBC Nova Scotia
Fernwood Publishing
Halifax Public Libraries

Other Funders and Supporters
Mount Saint Vincent University
    Nancy's Chair
Nova Scotia Black Educators
    Association
My Divine Appointment

Copyright © 2019 Global Afrikan Congress—Nova Scotia Chapter

All rights reserved. No part of this book may be reproduced or transmitted in any
form by any means without permission in writing from the publisher, except by
a reviewer, who may quote brief passages in a review.

Editor: Denise Gillard
Copy editor: Brenda Conroy
Interior design: John van der Woude, JVDW Designs
Cover design: Amina Abena Alfred, Araminta 5
Photos: Wanda Taylor and Sarah Taylor
Art photographer: Aaron Duncan
Printed and bound in Canada

Published by Roseway Publishing
an imprint of Fernwood Publishing
32 Oceanvista Lane, Black Point, Nova Scotia, B0J 1B0
and 748 Broadway Avenue, Winnipeg, Manitoba, R3G 0X3
www.fernwoodpublishing.ca/roseway

Fernwood Publishing Company Limited gratefully acknowledges the financial support of the
Government of Canada through the Canada Book Fund, the Canada Council for the Arts, the
Province of Nova Scotia and the Province of Manitoba for our publishing program.

Library and Archives Canada Cataloguing in Publication

Title: R is for reparations : young activists speaking their truth / Global Afrikan Congress—
    Nova Scotia Chapter.
Names: Global Afrikan Congress. Nova Scotia Chapter, sponsoring body.
Identifiers: Canadiana 20189067926 | ISBN 9781773632124 (softcover)
Subjects: LCSH: Slave trade—Africa. | LCSH: Reparations for historical injustices. |
    LCSH: Alphabet books.
Classification: LCC HT1322 .R17 2019 | DDC 382/.44096—dc23